WASTE MANAGEMENT

From Concept till Action Plan

BY NURBEK ACHILOV

ASTANA 2010

For questions and suggestions please contact: Mob.: +7(701)940-29-78, email: nurbek2020@gmail.com

Nurbek Achilov

WASTE MANAGEMENT: From Concept Till Action Plan, 2010

Translated and Adapted.
Translation by Google.com, 2019

1st Edition
ISBN: 9781095679463
All Rights Reserved

CONTENT

TABLES

FIGURES

LIST OF ABBREVIATIONS

AM	Automatic machines for receiving HIW
CB	Citizens and businesses - as sources of HIW
CL	Control
CT	Containers and tanks for HIW
D	Discounts
E	Enterprises - manufacturers of products and commodities, raw materials and materials
ER	Energy resources
FP	Factories and plants for processing of HIW
G	Government
HIWD	HIW dumps
HIW	Household and Industrial Waste
JSP	Joint social projects
M	Monitoring
MD	Media
MSW	Municipal solid waste
P	Privileges
PA	Preventive actions
PL	Penalties for placing HIW in the PND
PND	Places not designated for the release of HIW
R&D	Research and Development
PGRMS	Products and goods, raw materials and supplies
PR	Points of reception of HIW
PG	Products and goods
RM	Raw materials
RP	Research papers
SMA	Supervisory and Monitoring Authorities
SS	Subsidies
SV	Services
T	Taxes
WCPS	Waste of chemical power sources
WNM	Waste from natural materials
S	Summary
SIW	Solid industrial waste
SM	Shareholder management
SCST	Service of collection, sorting and transportation of HIW
TC	Trading companies (complexes)
$	Cash, Finance

INTRODUCTION

Creating an effective chain of recycling of household and industrial waste is one of the important steps in saving resources and obtaining benefits for the economy. It is important to learn the experience of the leading countries in Europe and other parts of the world, including Japan. As a result of the analysis of the world experience, an idea came to write a book about household and industrial waste (hereafter HIW) management, i.e. waste management. But to do it from concept part till the action plan.

In my opinion, we have to not only introduce what is already considered more efficient, but also introduce completely new results of the works of domestic and foreign scientists to implement larger-scale projects for the processing of HIW.

The offered concept of the book should stimulate:
1) creation of the mini plants for processing household and industrial waste in the regions;
2) starting of factories for the production of large and small machines, containers for various types of household and industrial waste;
3) building of transport infrastructure for the efficient transportation of HIW from the locations of containers to mini processing plants;
4) creation of value for HIW and gradually reducing the amount of HIW in the environment, bringing to zero;
5) a complete change in the thinking of the population around the world;
6) developing a new level of culture of the population in sorting HIW, its proper placement in containers, transportation and further processing;
7) improved R&D for efficient processing of HIW and further application in industry and in everyday life;
8) the creation of new infrastructure of the economy and new jobs;
9) improving the efficiency of usage for resource and making a profit from the implementation of the processes of recycled HIW around the world;
11) creation of a model for the transformation.

I believe that the implementation of the ideas of the book will allow our communities to achieve an innovative and waste-free economy, with a high level of per capita income and eventually develop regional economies of the world. It should motivate a reader for new business and public ideas.

Before proceeding to the disclosure of the concept, it is necessary to understand more thoroughly and deeper the HIW, to classify and segment the HIW.

I – HOUSEHOLD AND INDUSTRIAL WASTE

A) HIW CLASSIFICATION

In this part of the work, the classification and demonstration of various characteristics of HIW is carried out with the sole purpose to show the scale of the project and the priority implementation of the concept by stages of work.

In fact, in ordinary life, we are accustomed to seeing waste as the most unnecessary, averted and just refer to HIW simply "rubbish", from which you want to quickly get rid of, and go away. However, throwing off your "garbage" quickly, and sometimes throwing your "waste" in the street, we do not think at all about the value and a number of properties that negatively affect not only the environment, but and on the appearance of cities, and most importantly on the health of our citizens.

Only at the first stage of our small review of the environment, it is possible to segment HIW by values and by their effect on our environment. The table below shows the above with additional characteristics that are evident from an overview of the environment.

Table 1 Waste Classification

HIW	Option 1	Option 2	Option 3	Option 4
Reuse of HIW	Easily recycled HIW that can be used several times in the consumption cycle (bins, bottles)	Difficult to process HIW, requiring complete replacement of HIW parts or recycling (scrap metal, paper, glass)	Non-recyclable HIW	
The impact on the environment	Positive Impact (for example, tree leaves)	Negative influence (toxic chemicals, remnants of space, reactive objects)	Hazardous	
Weight	Light	Heavy	Super heavy	
Solid	Metals	Wood	Plastics	Glass
Liquid	Chemical	Biological	Mixed	
Gaseous	industrial (steam boiler)	toxic and toxic (emissions of enterprises)	turbine and car exhaust	
Mixed	food, human waste products	electrotechnical devices	industrial waste	
Radioactive	isotopes	metals	devices and	waste

			equipment	
Glass	Form	Color	Application	
Categories of the main HIW of the population	Glass products	Paper, cardboard	Plastic egg cakes, wrappers	Leftover food

It can be seen from the table that there are many varieties of HIW, which are very difficult to classify. A complexity of the classification is the main reason that in many countries processing of HIW is not importance and therefore remain the main problem of local societies. For proper classification, and most importantly, for effective work with subsequent sections of the concept, analysis of various sources of information, in particular, the Internet, was done.

Besides, in Germany and many other countries helped me to form a main understanding of the waste management systems.

For illustration, in one of the essays (without the author, 2001), on the Internet, the separation of solid industrial waste (hereinafter SIW) of engineering industries is shown, which were conventionally divided into two main groups:

1. SIW metal processing production units.
2. SIW of waste paper and packaging, which include cardboard, wrapping and other types of paper, waste wood shavings, sawdust from wood.

Further, the author of the abstract presents a classification of solid industrial (hereinafter SI) and household waste (hereinafter HW) in terms of physicochemical, biological, biochemical and toxicological properties.

According to the author, SIW should be divided into the following groups:

1. Waste of metal processing production units;
2. Waste of metallurgical production units;
3. Waste of glass and ceramic industries;
4. Waste in the production of polymeric materials of synthetic chemistry, including waste of rubber and rubber products;
5. Waste from natural polymeric materials, which include waste wood, cardboard, pulp and paper waste, waste fibroin, keratin, casein, collagen;
6. Waste of heating systems;
7. Fibrous waste;
8. Radioactive waste.

Further, the author points out that after solid waste, solid household waste (SHW) should be divided into the following groups.

A. Waste from natural materials (WNM)

1. Food or rotting waste.

2. Wastes of medical, medical, research organizations, including surgery and dentistry, as well as possibly waste medical veterinary institutions.

3. Polymer waste from natural materials, including waste wood, cardboard, pulp and paper, wrapping materials.

B. Industrial waste

1. Metal waste.

2. Waste of spent chemical current sources (WSCCS).

3. Fight glass and glassware.

4. Waste of polymeric materials of synthetic chemistry, including rubber and rubber products and all wrapping materials, and polymer packaging from products of synthetic chemistry.

5. Radioactive waste.

Regarding the classification of household waste and its proper handling, the information provided by the Japanese Center for the Management of General Safety (CMGS, 2009) provides an opportunity to see a complete picture of household waste. The table of this center is divided into the following columns: 1) sections; 2) types of waste; 3) a specific example; 4) notes; 5) collection and separation of waste.

Sections are divided into the following main groups:
1) Combustible waste, which includes food waste, wood products, boxes, clothing, etc.;
2) Non-combustible waste, which includes plastic products, polystyrene, aluminum foil, glass and ceramic products
3) Recyclable waste under number 2, which is collected by the relevant service after treatment (used paper products);
4) Recyclable waste number 1 (cans, plastic bottles, glass bottles);
5) Recyclable waste number 3, which is collected individually by the appropriate service after treatment (iron products, charging batteries, fluorescent lamps, cables, bricks, refractory materials);
6) Returned waste that is collected by the appropriate service after treatment (household appliances with a serial number and without a serial number);
7) Waste collected by manufacturers (cartridges).

From an analysis of recycling in Japan, we also saw that the country is very actively disposing part of the waste by incineration, which is a source of energy for heating for Japanese companies.

B) PROPOSED CLASSIFICATION SYSTEM

Based on the analysis and description of the HIW business chain, the following classification system for processing HIW is offered:
1) Food waste;
   a. Liquid;
   b. Solid.
2) Wood products;
   a. Furniture;
   b. Packaging;
   c. Products etc.
3) Clothes;
4) Plastic products (bottles, packages, vessels, etc.)
5) Products made of polyethylene or polystyrene;
   a. packages;

b. wrappers;
6) Aluminum foil products (packaging, food wrappers);
7) Glass;
8) Ceramics;
9) Crystal;
10) Tin cans for liquids;
    a. integers (for reuse);
    b. broken (for processing);
11) Plastic bottles (reuse);
12) Glass bottles;
13) Bottles for various reagents;
14) Paper
    a. Food packaging;
    b. Napkins;
15) Cardboard boxes;
16) Paper for printing various formats;
17) Magazines;
18) Newspapers;
19) Wrapping carton for containers;
20) Shredded paper;
21) Electric lamps;
22) Charging batteries of various sizes;
23) Developing films;
24) Cable cords and their parts;
25) Metal products;
    a. tin cans for various liquids and spray;
    b. wires;
    c. products;
    d. scrap metal
26) Cans and packaging;
    a. fuel;
    b. confectionery;
    c. jewelry, etc.
27) Bricks and cinder blocks;
28) Rubber products;
29) Plastic products;
30) Mechanical and electrical devices (with serial number);
    a. equipment;
    b. air conditioners;
    c. computers;
    d. clock;
    e. phones, printers, refrigerators, etc.
31) Cars and other vehicles;
32) Additional devices (without serial number)
    a. speakers;
    b. headphones;
    c. antennas;
33) Cartridges.
34) Biological HIW

35) Chemical HIW
   a. instruments and tools;
   b. substances;
   c. oil;
36) Medical HIW;
   a. disposable syringes;
   b. tools and devices;
   c. operational outlets;
37) Radioactive HIW;
   a. devices and equipment;
   b. substances;
38) Bacteriological and poisonous HIW
   a. devices and equipment;
   b. substances.

Generally, every country should learn how to classify waste to many groups. This will allow societies to effectively sort the garbage and earn additional capital.

C) DESCRIPTION OF WORK WITH HIW

According to the proposed system of classification, the following table is offered to show the characteristic of working with various types of HIW according to the purposes of collection, circulation and collection.

Table 2 Characteristic of working with various types of HIW

#	HIW	Purpose of collection	Handling	Collection
1	Food	for incineration	Required to wrap in plastic packaging	containers with special designation (A) and color (Black)
2	Wood products	for incineration or restoration		containers with specials designation (B) and color (Brown), or reception points 1
3	Cloths	For incineration, or for persons in need	Require processing when transferring to another person or selling	reception points 1, containers (C) and color (Blue)
4	Plastic products	For smelting and processing		containers (D) and color (White), receiving points 1
5	Polyethylene or polystyrene products	For smelting and processing		reception points 1, containers (D) and color (White)
6	Aluminum Foil Products	Broken glass (by color), cans		reception points 1
7	Broken glass (by	Broken glass (by	Must be cleaned of	special containers

#				
	color), cans	color), cans	dirt	(D) and (Green), reception points 1
8	Ceramics	For processing		reception points 1
9	Crystal	For processing		reception points 1
10	Tin cans for liquid			
	without scathe	For processing		Reception points 2, vending machines, shopping centers
	broken	For smelting and processing		Containers (E) and color (Orange), receiving points
11	Plastic egg caps	For processing		Reception points 2, vending machines, shopping centers
12	Glass Bottles	For processing		Reception points 2, vending machines, shopping centers
13	Bottles for various reagents	For smelting and processing		Reception points 5
14	Paper			
	Food packaging, napkins	For incineration, processing		Containers (B), reception points 1
15	Carton boxes	For processing		
16	paper for printing in various formats	For processing		Reception points 1, Containers (B)
17	Magazines	For processing		
18	Newspapers	For processing		
19	Wrapping carton for containers			
20	Shredded paper			Containers (B), reception points 1
21	Lamps	For shipment to the manufacturer		Reception points 3
22	Charging batteries	For shipment to the manufacturer		Reception points 3
23	Developing films	For shipment to the manufacturer		Reception points 3
24	Cable cords and parts thereof	For shipment to the manufacturer		Reception points 3
25	Metalwork	For smelting and processing		Containers (F), Reception points 1,
26	Jars and packaging	For shipment to the manufacturer		Reception points 3
27	Bricks and cinder blocks			Reception points 1
28	Rubber products	For processing		Reception points 1,

				Containers (G)
29	Plastic products	For smelting and processing		Containers (D), Reception points 1
30	Mechanical and electrical devices	For parsing, processing, or shipment to the manufacturer		Reception points 3
31	Cars and other vehicles	For parsing, processing, or shipment to the manufacturer		Reception points 4
32	Add. appliances	For parsing and processing		Reception points 3
33	Cartridges	For shipment to the manufacturer		Reception points 3
34	Biological HIW	For shipment, melting and processing		Reception points 5
35	Chemical HIW	For shipment, melting and processing		Reception points 6
36	Medical HIW	For shipment, melting and processing		Reception points 5
37	Radioactive HIW	For shipment, melting and processing		Reception points 6
38	Bacteriological and poisonous HIW	For shipment, melting and processing		Reception points 5

From the table it is clear that the containers and reception points have different numbering and letter designations. In this case, it means that different types of containers and tanks will be required for different types of HIW, and different types of points of reception of HIW will also be required.

D) CONCLUSIONS AND RECOMMENDATIONS

The main conclusions of the classification are:

1) Analysis of articles on the processing of HIW in the world show that there is no single system of classification, and even more for the utilization and processing of HIW. This is one of the main sources, which shows the discrepancy in the management of HIW in the world and thereby shows the inefficiency of the world management system of HIW. In each country, the cheapest method of disposal and recycling is chosen.

2) For a more detailed classification of HIW and in the future for implementation of an investment project, it is necessary to analyze the main HIW in the region.

3) In order to implement the project successfully, motivating world community and turning into a global action, it is necessary to analyze the following factors:
- sources of HIW;
- a process chain of HIW: collection points, warehousing, transportation, processing, and sales to consumers of the final results of HIW processing;
- analysis of processing plants, points of collection and reception of HIW, transport services;
- promotion chain of social and environmental advertising in the media, outdoor advertising and political propaganda;
- analysis of the cost and payback of projects.

4) In 1993, in order to promote household waste processing and sorting, the Minamata City Administration, Japan (Minamata City Administration, 2009) planned a detailed waste classification system; Waste was categorized into 21 categories in 1999, and into 23 categories in 2000. From this it follows that for the gradual and effective implementation of the HIW processing system it may not be immediately necessary to determine the exact classification system. This will depend on the cost of organizing an effective chain of business for receiving, transporting and processing of the HIW.

5) The experience of introducing a separate waste collection system in the five federal states of the Federal Republic of Germany shows that the education of the population (including educational work in kindergartens, schools, vocational and higher educational institutions and promoting the need for separate waste collection in the media) 70% of the funds were spent, on the creation of a system (a clear structure capable of efficiently behaving with waste) - 20%, on solving technical problems (introduction of efficient waste treatment technologies) - 10% (Suprunenko O., 2001). Consequently, for the analysis and classification of HIW, it is also necessary to analyze and plan the budget for education of the population, the structure of the system, technologies and solutions for recycling.

E) INFORMATION SOURCES

[1] Minimata City Administration (2009), "Guide model of ecological city "section" classification and recycling", Extracted June 24, 2009 from: http://www.minamatacity.jp/eng/mec/mec_friendly_living.htm#

[2] Without Author (2001), Translation: "Classification of solid industrial and household waste", essay, extracted June 23, 2009 from: http://www.studzona.com/referats/view/1486

[3] Oleg Suprunenko (2001), "The Garbage Era: From Dawn to Dusk", Mirror of the Week, No. 34 (358) September 1 - 7, 2001, taken on June 24, 2009 from: http://www.zerkalo-nedeli.com/3000/3320/32051/

[4] Center for General Security Management (CGSM, 2009), "Waste classification table", extracted June 23, 2009 from: www.gsmc.titech.ac.jp/.../haikibutu%20bunbetuichiran%20english.pdf

II – HIW BUSINESS CYCLE MOVEMENT

In order to organize the effective classification and implementation of the innovative system of professional education, it is necessary to clearly present the entire business cycle of education of professional education. After the initial review of the business cycle, you can proceed to a more detailed description of the stages and the initial developments of the financial business model.

The following figure represents the standard business cycle for HIW.

Figure 1 HIW Business Cycle

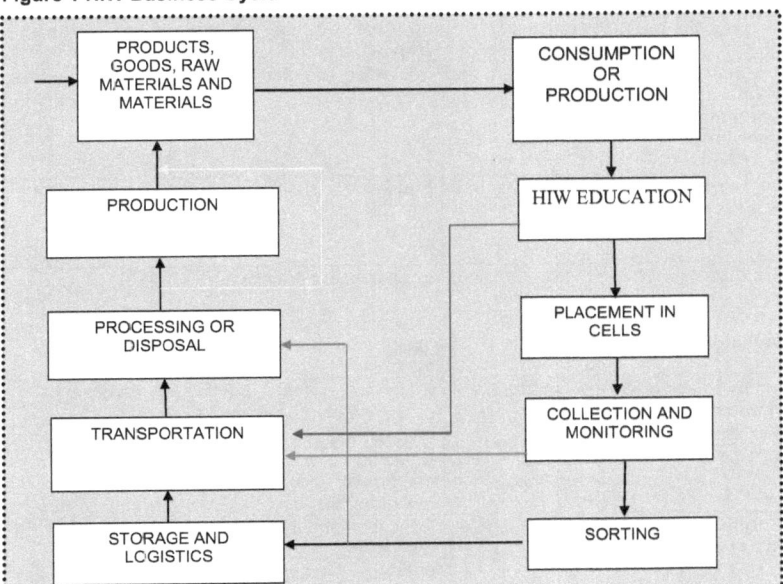

The figure shows that, according to the initial analysis, the business cycle consists of 10 stages. To build an effective business cycle, it is necessary to take into account many other features of the region and the formation of HIW over time.

Further, we would like to briefly reveal the features of the stages and supplement them with new features. This would create a value at every stage and save our resources and time. For the business cycle to become effective, it is necessary to pay attention to creating benefits in each chain of business and, at the same time, determine which measures need to be constantly carried out in order not to set the cyclical nature of the problems that arise.

One of the important requirements of the system is the flexibility of the business chain structure, that is, the business chain should be built depending on the type of HIW (See the figure above. The structure of the various business cycles is marked with colored lines). This allows you to reduce unnecessary processes and promptly deliver HIW for recycling.

It should be noted that the system of movement of HIW is not new. The main goal of this work is the creation of a universal system of movement of the HIW, which could be easily adapted in various developing and neighboring countries.

Next, we consider a table in which a brief description of the stages of the business cycle is presented.

Table 3 Stages of HIW business cycle and its characteristics

	Efficiency	Investment for improvement of working with HIW	Participants
Products and goods, raw materials and supplies (PGRMS)	Decrease in the share of defective or damaged units	Education and training	Producers, trade, households
Consumption and Production	Economical and prudent use of PGRMS	Education and training	Producers, trade, households, population, youth, children
Creation of HIW	Proper handling of various HIW	Education and training	All
Placing in cells/boxes	Proper placement in cells	Education and training, tanks, containers and materials	All
Collection and monitoring of HIW cells	Reduction in the proportion of errors	Education and training, transportation, equipment, raw materials	Enterprise 1
Sorting	Reduction in the proportion of errors	Education and training, equipment, energy, raw materials	Enterprise 1
Warehousing and storage	Optimal use of space	Education and training, equipment, energy, transport, raw materials and materials	Enterprise 1
Transportation	Efficient, just-in-time service and transportation system	Trainings, transport, fuel, raw materials	Enterprise 1
Processing or recycling	Efficient processing	Education and training, equipment, transport, energy, raw materials and materials	Enterprise 2
Production at enterprises	Снижение доли брака и порчи	Education and training	Producers, trade, households

16

This table shows the following characteristics of the stages of the business cycle: 1) the effectiveness of the work that needs to be done in each chain of the business cycle; 2) investment in major events and procurement; 3) Active participants and objects of the main event.

Despite the fact that the table gives a broad understanding of the issues that need to be solved, it practically lacks the motivating factors that would make the system and its participants work in perspective. It should be noted that in many countries, including developed countries, the processing of HIW is subsidized and financed by the state.

In general, if we take it, the HIW system would have to work equally in all countries, since the state is the main distributor of the budget for the processing of HIW. In developing countries, the system does not work, not only because the states have very small budgets for HIW, but mainly because of the high degree of corruption, low level of education of the population about HIW.

In developed countries, where companies save on every cent, the main motivating factor for the population and the company is that, for example, people and organizations receive money or various types of benefits for the HIW. In addition, many sectors of the economy and business areas are involved in the projects.

We know that the main goal of any economic activity is to make a profit, and at the same time, many of us forget that activity should be aimed at reducing costs and improving the environment where we live and work. This is precisely the fundamental fact that in developed countries, companies and the state are actively working on socially-oriented measures and projects, including reducing HIW in the environment. If you take each socially-oriented event, the important question is: how many times will the costs and damage be reduced to the state and the enterprise in the future, if held, this or that event for the population today. Thus, enterprises constantly and purposefully invest part of their income in the development of socially-oriented projects. As a result, losing small incomes at the present time, companies increase their chances of obtaining permanent and growing incomes in the future. This is mainly due to the positive mood of the population and the positive atmosphere of the environment.

Returning to the topic of creating an effective system for processing and recycling household waste, it is necessary that companies producing products and goods, as well as raw materials and materials (hereinafter referred to as PGRMS), provide a small portion of their income, for example, to purchase HIW from the population and organization. Another option is if part of the proceeds will be spent on the purchase of PGRMS from refinery HIW plants. Thus, in the chain of movement of the HIW to create a factor of motivation for the population or organization, which provide a constant effective circulation PGRMS and HIW.

An alternative option may be the situation when manufacturing companies of goods and products will be cheaper to purchase raw materials and materials from the company collecting or processing HIW.

Summarizing the above questions, we would like to show the system of motivation for the three categories of participants in the HIW system in the table below. The Table 4 identifies the following participants: 1) creators or sources of HIW; 2) enterprises in the business cycle of HIW; 3) the government.

Table 4 List of Motivators for participants of the HIW business cycle

	Creators of HIW	Enterprises in the business cycle of HIW movement	Government
Motivation 1	Receipt of income for the transfer of HIW at a certain time or in a certain place	Receipt of income for each unit or volume of HIW	Reduced budget for maintaining cleanliness and order
Motivation 2	Saving time	Efficient sorting by those who create HIW	Increase revenue due to company activities
Motivation 3	Cash savings	Saving time	Creation of new jobs
Motivation 4	Receiving discounts and benefits	Saving energy and resources	Ensuring the improvement of environmental, sanitary and medical indicators
Motivation 5	Ease of use in any setting	Creating loyal customers of PGRMS consumers	Improving living standards and incomes
Motivation 6	Cleanliness and tidiness	Revenue increase	Improving social performance

The Table 4 shows that each participant in the HIW business cycle has 6 benefits or motivating factors that are not limited to this.

It is important that each participant in the business cycle be aware of the motivating factors or benefits to the extent that work and livelihood processes are constantly improved. Perhaps, the benefits will not be immediately clear to the participants, but with the help of the media, youth, social and political links, certain results can be achieved in a short period of time. If 30 - 50 percent of the population are aware of the effects of motivating factors, the system will automatically and independently start working on improvement.

As noted earlier, addressing motivation issues require building a financial model of a business chain. Only then it will be possible to attract participants to work on the implementation of the project and only in this way it will be possible to get the desired financial result for each participant.

III – FINANCIAL MODEL

In this section of the book, the models of movement of finance and HIW between various participants of the HIW business chain will be described. Without a financial model, as noted earlier, not every participant will be interested in such a large-scale project. Whatever the project or business plan, it should contain production and financial models. This will avoid various conflicts between the participants, and most importantly do not allow the project to stop working half way, redistributing responsibility to each other.

To build a financial model of the concept, it is necessary to identify the main interacting participants first. Let's enumerate them and label them for convenience.

1) Citizens and businesses who take out HIW (hereinafter **CB**);
2) The service of collection, sorting, transportation of HIW (hereinafter **SCST**);
3) Trading companies (hereinafter **TC**);
4) Enterprises (hereinafter **E**);
5) HIW factories and plants (hereinafter **FP**);
6) Supervisory and monitoring authorities (hereinafter referred to as **SMA**);
7) Government (hereinafter referred to as **G**);
8) Automatic machines for taking HIW in (hereinafter the **AM**);
9) Containers and tanks for HIW (hereinafter referred to as **CT**);
10) HIW reception points (hereinafter **PR**);
11) landfill or disposal sites (**HIWD**). After reaching the desired level of system operation and quality of processing, all HIWD will be closed.
12) places not allowed for the release of HIW (**PND**).

Next, select the objects of the movement and the relationship between the participants:

1) cash, finance (hereinafter **$**);
2) household and industrial waste (hereinafter **HIW**);
3) penalties (hereinafter **PL**);
4) privileges (hereinafter **P**);
5) discounts (hereinafter **D**);
6) raw materials and materials (hereinafter **RM**);
7) products and goods (hereinafter **PG**);
8) energy resources (hereinafter **ER**);
9) taxes (hereinafter **T**);
10) subsidies (hereinafter **SS**);
11) summary (further **S**);
12) monitoring (hereinafter **M**);
13) services (hereinafter **SV**);
14) joint social projects (hereinafter **JSP**);
15) preventive actions (hereinafter **PA**);
16) shareholder management (hereinafter **SM**);
17) control (hereinafter referred to as **C**).

In addition, it is necessary to allocate as an object - the place that is not intended for the release of the HIW (hereinafter **PND**). For the release of HIW in the wrong place, state supervisory authorities and special services for the collection of HIW should be monitored, and when they discover that a deliberate waste is released, they must discipline citizens and enterprises by issuing fines and other measures provided by the legislation.

Places, which are not for release of HIW, should be understood as any other place in the environment, except for places or cells (containers, tanks, points) intended for HIW. This applies both in the city, in the countryside, and of course in the moving objects.

Supervisors should not only monitor and review violations, but mainly engage in preventive measures both among the population, the youth, and in enterprises.

Figure 2 Financial Model

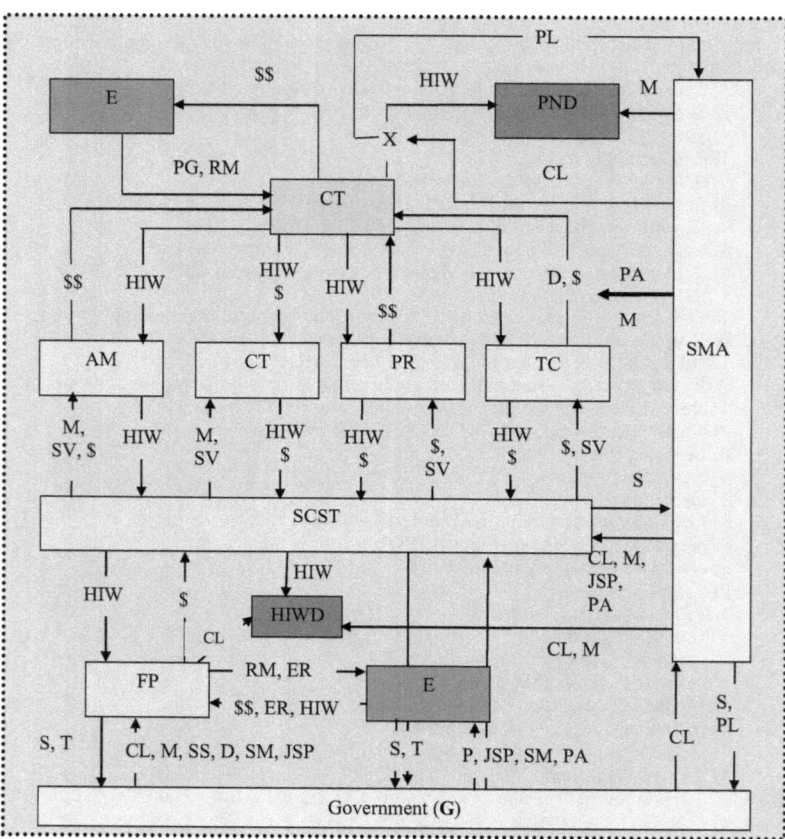

For the convenience of understanding the financial model, we will use "arrows" that will describe the movement of objects and relationships, and "rectangular squares" that will show the participants in the model. It should be noted that for the effective operation of

20

the system, it is necessary to create flexibility for both the sources of HIW (population and enterprise), and for enterprises operating in the business cycle of HIW and state regulatory bodies.

Thus, the Figure 2 represents the overall financial model.

The figure shows not only the financial model of the system, but also a partially partial production model with HIW. A more detailed disclosure of links and objects of the system is of more important interest and the subject of the next section "production model".

Further I will try to disclose models of the HIW system, i.e. descriptions of production (operational), marketing, and technological models.

IV – PRODUCTION MODEL

The processes and mechanisms of work between each participant in the HIW system will be described in the production model, i.e. in this part of the book. For convenience and a clearer understanding of the work of each participant among themselves, each relationship between the participants will explained in separate sections.

In this section, we begin with the very first stage of the relationship between the "buyer", designated "**CB**" and "seller", designated "**E**" in the figure of the previous section. Next, consider the rest gradually.

RELATIONSHIP BETWEEN ENTERPRISES AND CITIZENS AND BUSINESS

Let's consider the relationship between the first two participants in the figure 3 below.

Figure 3 Relationship of E-CB

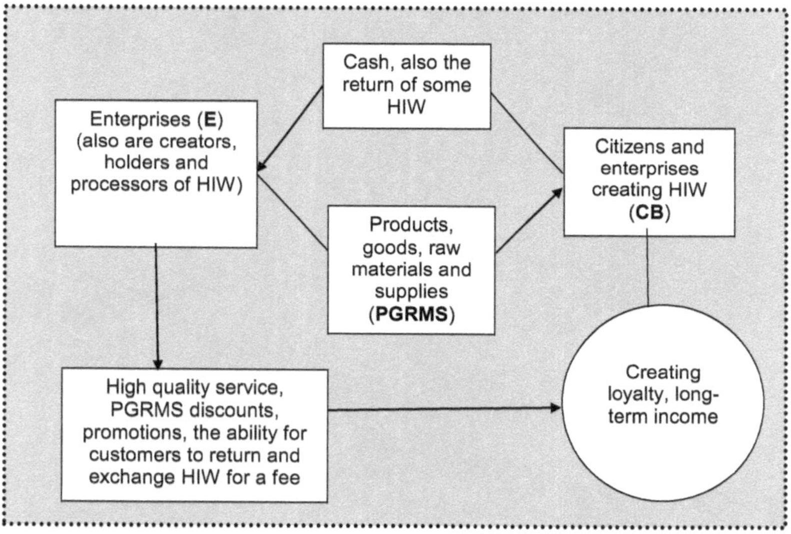

It is clear from the figure 3 that the main goal of the enterprises should be not only generation of income through the production and sale of PGRMS, but also creation of customer loyalty and reduction of costs by processing some HIW inhouse, that is, within the enterprise.

Returning to the topic of HIW, the question arises about which HIW can buy or exchange enterprises from customers (through their sales representatives or directly) and process them within the enterprise, and which HIW will go to processing to HIW plants and factories directly through the SCST.

For example, enterprises selling various beverages in plastic or glass containers should provide through which network empty containers will be returned to their enterprises. Through special sorting services for collection of HIW or through a network of retail supermarkets where special automatic machines for collecting containers are installed, or shopping centers, which can exchange containers and deduct the cost of containers from buyers' purchased goods.

Let us see on factors that can make an organization of a HIW network work for enterprises.

1) The amount of investment for setting up the processing network of some HIW in the enterprise.
2) Investment profitability and payback. If this activity is not profitable, then it is better to provide specialized factories and plants.
3) Research base. HIW is always a mixture of different materials and elements. To get the necessary product, raw materials and materials from HIW require highly skilled researchers and testers who could tell exactly which HIW may be suitable for processing and what volumes are needed. In addition, it would be clear what time and resource expenditures are needed to derive the necessary RM, or just energy. The result of the research work (hereinafter R&D) can be a product that will require patenting, and so a new R&D product can be very popular and economical in the market.
4) Infrastructure or network collection and transportation. The organization of the traffic network and mutual settlements requires modern information and communication and transport networks, both information processing and the physical movement of HIW. Enterprises must calculate whether the sales representatives of an enterprise should collect HIW or whether new services companies should do this.
5) The volume of the market at home and abroad. In the future, it will be possible to process HIW in other countries or build HIW plants and factories for processing and generating income in other countries.

AUTOMATIC MACHINES (AM)

In many developed countries such as in Germany and Japan, HIW automatic machines are a very convenient collection system for many and valuable kind of HIW in everyday life and industry.

For example, automatic machines can collect glass and plastic bottles, batteries and other valuable items.

To understand, consider the relationship CB-AM system in the figure 4:

Figure 4 Relationship of CB-AM

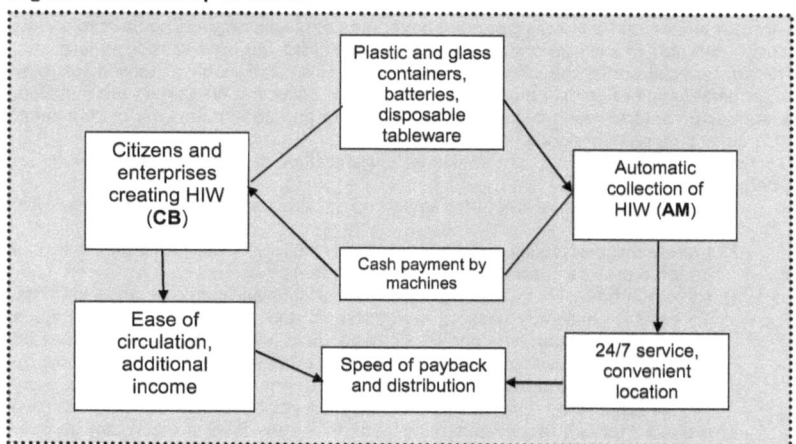

For the introduction of machines for collection of HIW in the economy, a company should answer on the following issues:

1) the cost of manufacturing machines;
2) determining the types of HIW that will be collected with the help of machines and will be effective and profitable for further processing;
3) identification of machine owners (maintenance, monitoring and control);
4) determination of pricing for the collection of HIW and payback of machines;
5) determination of locations (residential areas, supermarkets, hypermarkets, etc.);
6) the possible export of automatic machines to the near and far abroad.

CONTAINERS AND TANKS (CT)

Containers and tanks designed to collect HIW are the most common and traditional system for collecting HIW from the population and enterprises.

The only difference between developed and developing countries is in culture of throwing waste into the containers and tanks. In developed countries, they learned how to separate garbage and put them in certain tanks and containers. In developing countries, unfortunately, people throw their garbage in one container or tank.

The causes and results for throwing HIW without separation are the following circumstances and facts:

1) The places where the containers and tanks for HIW placed are heavily polluted, has an unpleasant appearance, and also rotting HIW quickly spread odors over distances.

2) Basically, such HIW is very difficult to sort further (time and resource consuming), and therefore HIW are transported to city landfills for incineration or burial. Wherein it does not take into account which environmental effects of the products of combustion or decomposition of

HIW have on the environment, soil, groundwater, and ultimately on people.

3) Due to the lack of an effective monitoring and management system, HIWs are transported over various periods. In some places, places with containers and tanks turn into huge dumps.

4) The lack of a unified electronic information system (unified city surveillance cameras, electronic complaints system) and quality standards for container and tank locations (in terms of cleanliness, sanitary standards, number of tanks per population, number of transportations, etc.) lead to violations of quality and purity.

5) Due to the poor appearance of the locations for containers and tanks, and of course dumps, the population and the companies have very negative attitudes towards the service companies, involved in the maintenance, transport and processing of HIW.

6) Negative attitude is also caused by the types of transport on which HIW is transported. The main lorry fleet of service companies is very outdated and due to low quality requirements, most vehicles do not undergo periodic sanitary cleaning and washing.

7) Since some HIWs have value and are accepted at some receiving points for further fusion or processing, the collectors of valuable HIW from containers and tanks are people who collect HIW to obtain small amounts of money for their living. On the other hand, such people are perceived by the public very badly.

8) The problem is that there is a lack of a sufficient number of processing shops, factories and enterprises that require certain investments. The main factor of limited investment in this area is the lack of value and value of HIW. If enterprises processing HIW do not know where to market the results of processing as raw materials, it is very difficult to build an effective network of processing HIW. Thus, this issue requires a research decision by the enterprises.

9) Since HIW is not classified and there is no agreement between manufacturers and HIW-processing plants and factories, the issues of forming an effective business chain are becoming more complex. The following actions are necessary for separate submission of the HIW by enterprises and the public: marking future HIW by enterprises, coordination of this labeling system with participants of the HIW business chain; active training of the population and the company to determine the labeling and proper placement in containers and tanks; training of staff in the proper sorting and transportation of HIW on the basis of labeling. When importing goods and products from abroad, the labeling requirement must apply to importing enterprises, which only after proper laboratory examination of the quality standards committee must receive a classification system label and permission to import goods and products.

10) In addition, for the release of HIW in certain containers and efficient transportation, certain requirements are necessary. For example, in Germany for the discharge of empty glass jars of different colors, there are various iron containers. Before placing the glass jars in color in different containers, the jars should be cleaned and separated from the

lids. Covers are placed in separate tanks. For violation of the rules for the placement of HIW in Germany strict penalties can apply for companies and citizens. In order to effectively accommodate HIW by the population, especially the younger generation or non-residents of the country, appropriate preventive and educational programs should be conducted.

11)   In general, there are no courses or lessons on HIW in educational institutions. This is the most important factor in the indifference of the population to the process of determining HIW, proper placement and, in general, understanding the influence and threats of HIW on the environment and cleanliness. In this regard, it is useful to introduce introductory and compulsory lessons already at the first stage of the project in kindergartens, schools and universities.

Figure 5 Creation of HIW in Trade Center

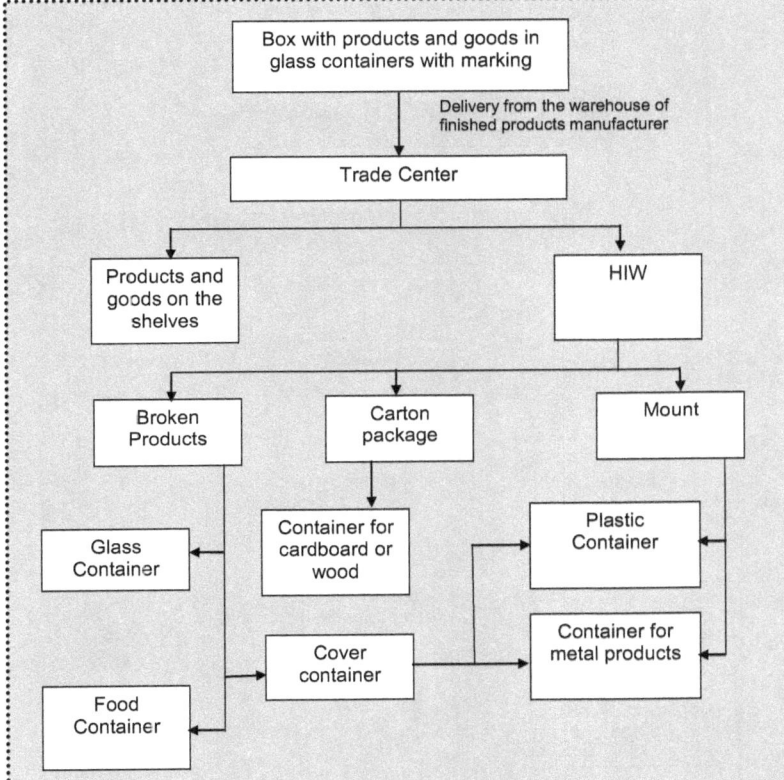

12)   At the present time, in many countries, the population will pay small amount of money for the removal of HIW. Billing of HIW exportation is mainly determined by the cost method, i.e. a method that covers the transportation and administrative costs of enterprises exporting HIW to landfills in the city. With this method, none of the participants feel responsibility for economy and ecology in the business chain.

Figure 6 Example of Formation of HIW by Consumer

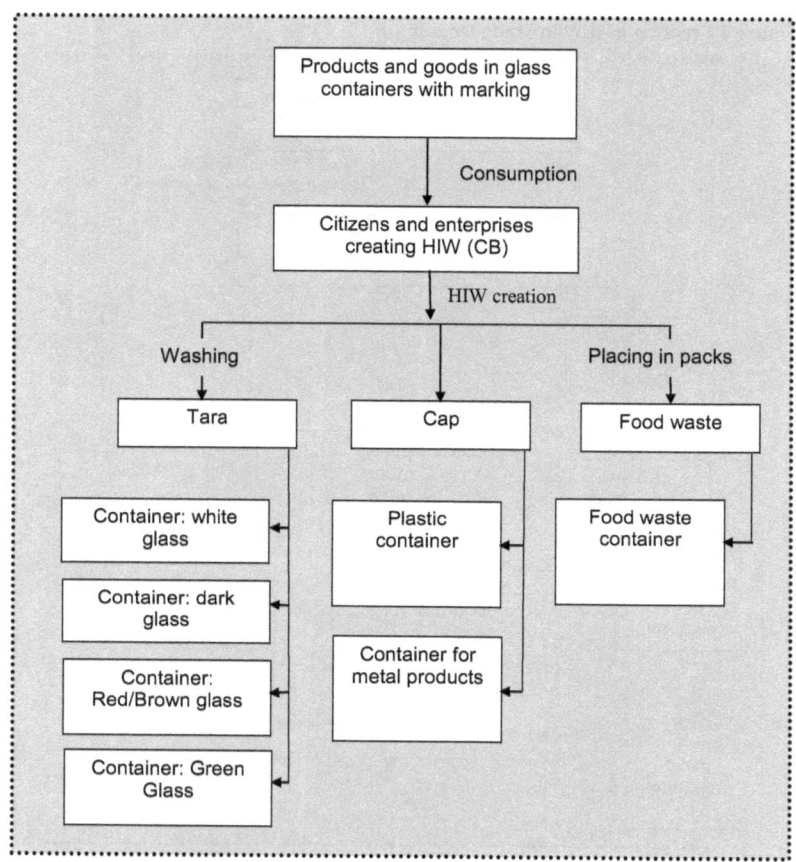

In general, the solution of the system of questions requires a huge investment of time and resources, covers the solution of a wide range of issues of all sectors of the economy, and requires active educational activities of the population and enterprises, and of course, media, political parties, government and non-government public organizations.

Let us further consider in the Figure 5 the process of development of HIW in the process of selling products and goods in glass containers with marking (the marking will be considered in the following chapters). Consider the case of HIW at the mall.

The Figure 5 shows what possible HIW can be formed in the shopping centers during the sales of food in glass containers.

For the same products, we now look at the Figure 6, but for the final consumers of the products.
It should be noted that this synthesis process makes it possible to see that the main container, which is used for delivery from the warehouse of finished products of the manufacturer, will practically not reach the final consumer. This suggests that enterprises can reduce their costs for the design and exterior design of the main packaging, which is delivered to shopping centers, and concentrate the advertising look and design on the product for the final consumer and the design of the awning of cargo transport vehicles.

The main container of delivery to the shopping center can be reusable, made of plastic or metal, for example, upon receipt of an application from retail outlets, the manufacturer of beverages, for example, Coca-Cola exchanges realized empty boxes for full boxes of beverages. In such a case, the container may be framed and used until a certain amount of wear.

From the Figure 6, it can be seen that buying food in glassware is the source of three types of HIW for the consumer: 1) glass containers; 2) a cover, which may be plastic or metal; 3) food waste.
The Figure 6 shows that different containers are used for different colors of glass containers. The same could be done for plastic products, which can be based not only on the chemical and biological properties of HIW products, but mainly on the generally accepted classification of HIW and the accepted labeling of an enterprise for products, goods, raw materials and materials.

HIW RECEPTION POINTS (RP)
The interaction of the following participants plays an important role for difficult-to-determine HIW and when the large amounts of HIW are generated in one factory or unit. Points of acceptance of HIW are the points of sorting and distribution of HIW according to classification and for further processing at the respective plants.

Let's consider the interaction of two participants in the Figure 7.
It can be seen from the Figure 7 that the effective functioning of HIW reception points (hereinafter PR) depends on a number of important factors, both on the part of the CB to create their trust and the internal organization of the PR.

Figure 7 A Model of Interaction of CB and PR

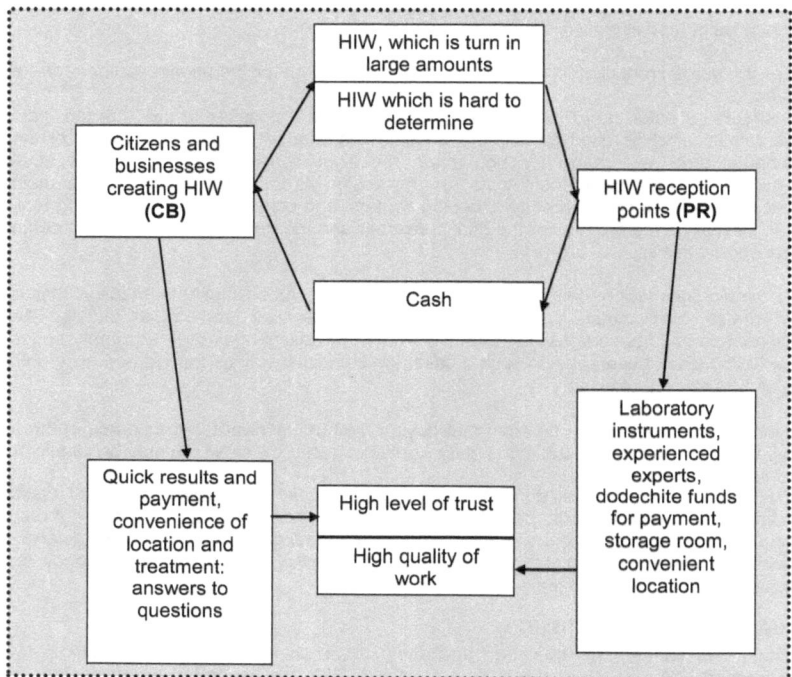

Since the receiving points will pay large sums and accept products that are difficult to determine by value, the procedure for evaluating and classifying the HIW is important for the effective operation of the PR. In addition, due to the fact that a large number of the population has difficulties with determining the chemical and other properties of HIW for their proper placement, it is also important that the reception points in cities and rural areas are located.

With the effective organization of transport services and logistics system for the transportation of HIW, the factor of the availability of storage space has a less significant role. As huge warehouses can increase the cost of maintenance and operation.

Points of reception of HIW should have a very developed system of cash desks for the payment of money to consumers on the delivered HIW. These poinyd can also play the role of consulting centers by phone. If difficulties arise in determining HIW or transportation, points of reception of HIW, the experts of the centers should properly advise citizens and employees of the enterprise.

The following Figure 8 shows the types of work that can provide PR to the population and enterprises.

Figure 8 Activities of Point of Reception

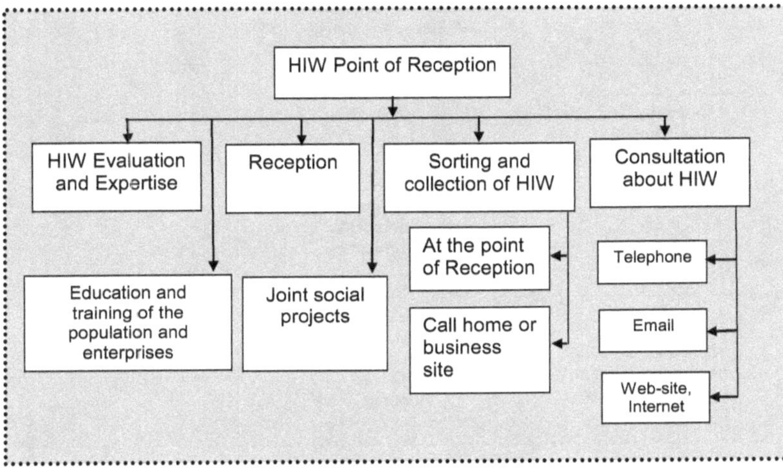

The Figure 8 shows that the HIW reception points will play an important role in servicing the population and enterprises. This link of the business chain will directly implement the quality work of the primary chain of activities with clients, and if necessary, assist in the assessment and examination, acceptance, sorting, transportation and additional consultations at a convenient time for the population and the enterprise. Points of acceptance of the HIW will additionally conduct training for the population and enterprises on the culture of handling HIW, the rules of placement. Together with local and higher state bodies, this unit will carry out social projects for the development of infrastructure services for the population and enterprises.

TRADING COMPANIES (TC)

Trading companies (hereinafter referred to as TC) sell products and goods of manufacturing companies and are one of the four main participants in the HIW business cycle.

Consider in the Figure 9 the interaction of TC in the business cycle for efficiency chain of HIW services.

Figure 9 Interaction of TC in HIW business cycle

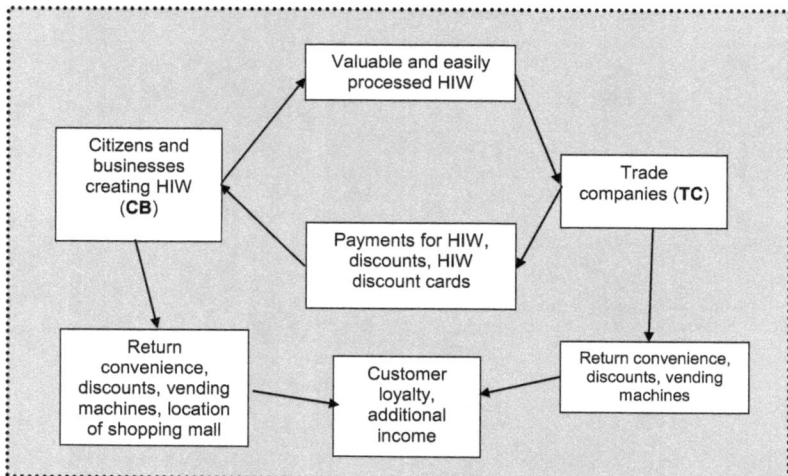

Figure 9 shows that the result of accepting valuable and easily processed HIW from citizens and enterprises is the preservation of customer loyalty and the opportunity to receive additional income.

The benefits for the trading company are furthermore in concluding their contracts with manufacturers and HIW processing plants. Here, TC can receive certain discounts from manufacturers, or TC can profitably pass HIW to processing companies.

SERVICES OF COLLECTION, SORTING AND TRANSPORTATION (SCST)

The service of collection, sorting and transportation of HIW (hereinafter referred to as SCST) plays an important role in ensuring the speed, mobility and efficiency of interaction in the HIW business chain.

After the initial collection and sorting of such units as AM, CT, PR, and TC, this service provides further collection and sorting, and further transportation to the places of destination of HIW: 1) processing plants and factories; 2) in the shops of industrial production enterprises.

This service provides not only HIW transportation from own HIW accommodation facilities, but also provides services to third companies in sorting and transporting HIW. Consider the relationship of the SCST in the Figure 10 below.

Figure 10 Relationship of SCST

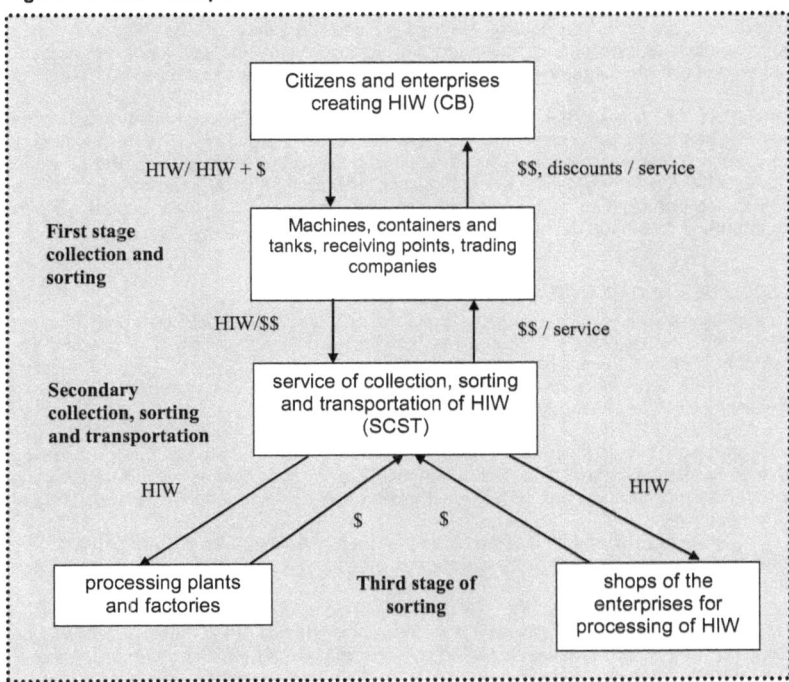

It can be seen from the Figure 10 that SCST play an enormous role in the secondary collection, sorting and transportation of HIW, not directly from the CB, but through machines, containers and tanks, receiving points and trading companies. The last objects perform the work on the primary collection and sorting of HIW.

The effectiveness and efficiency of the work of the SCST depends largely on the activities of facilities for the primary assembly and sorting of HIW. Therefore, an important goal of the SCST is to promote social measures for the proper handling and placement of HIW, as well as measures for cleanliness and order, greening and improving the domestic climate.

Since the activity of the SCST plays an important role in maintaining cleanliness and order in regions, it is necessary to constantly monitor and analyze work data, as well as create an effective system of supervision of the SCST for work and maintenance.

In general, the SCST should provide daily reports to the supervisory authorities, which in turn should be monitored through a single system of reports and bulletins and identify violations of the SCST. All statistics (daily, weekly, monthly, quarterly, annual) on servicing the objects of collection and sorting of HIW should be available to the population and government bodies through the Internet.

In addition, in order to quickly respond to the demands of the population and government agencies on the placement and sorting of HIW, as well as on problematic issues, special headings or a forum should be created to discuss these issues via the Internet.

The SCST, being a subject of market relations and a joint-stock company counting on income, has the right to receive government benefits and subsidies. The introduction of new technologies on an ongoing basis requires large capital expenditures and scientific research, which are sometimes only possible for the state or large companies. In this regard, the participation of the state and large companies in the share capital will play an important role in the development of the HIW chain.

FACTORIES AND PLANTS (FP)

This relationship is discussed in the previous paragraph. It should be noted that the relationship between the SCST and the FP can be built with a variety of options. For example, consider several of them:

1) FP can be located in each area one by one. In this case, the SCST can transport HIW independently.

2) one FP can be located for several regions. In this case, the SCST can transport the HIW independently, if the distance is not so remote. Or transport by special train, which may be owned by the SCST or by third parties. When transporting with the help of third parties, SCST must provide the necessary tightness and safety of cargo and HIW.

3) Some FPs may be located alone per country. In this case SCSTs can also use their own transport or third parties. Depends on the cost of each type of transport and distance.

4) Some workshops of the FPs can be located in large settlements.

From the above points it follows that for different types of HIW, different FPs will be created. They will be created depending on the volumes of HIW in a certain period of time and of course certain investment costs for creating FP and processing HIW.

The relationship between the FP and E should be free-market in nature. How can we build an effective network, in our case? There are several options:

1) Enterprises create HIW, which they can transport to the FP and then receive energy resources, raw materials or materials, and cash from the FP.

2) Enterprises can buy from the FP their processed HIW in the form of raw materials.

3) Enterprises can buy sterilized and recycled production materials from the FP for the manufacture of finished products.

4) Enterprises can buy energy resources from the FP.

5) If the research departments of the FP can develop semi-finished or finished products and products, then E can buy to produce finished products for the final consumer.

6) FPs can also exchange and buy energy resources from E, for processing HIW

Next, consider the Figure 11 - the relationship between the FP and E.

Figure 11 Relationship between FP and E

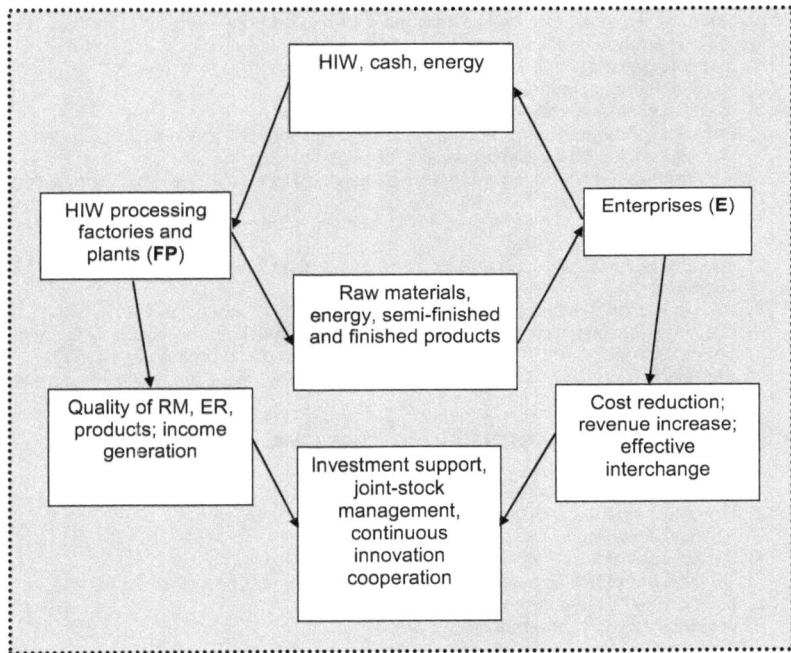

The Figure 11 shows that the effectiveness of the FP depends on the quality of the provided RM, ER and products, and, ultimately, income. At the same time, efficiency for enterprises will be a reduction in costs due to the purchase of cheaper resources and an increase in profitability. The result of effective interchange can be investment support, equity management, and innovative collaboration.

GOVERNMENT (G)

The state is the main participant and initiator of activities related to the creation of a highly efficient and constantly evolving system for processing HIW.

Benefits for the state as a result of building the system will be:

1) providing employment to the population in the new processing industry;

2) receipt of income in the form of taxes;
3) reducing the cost of creating cleanliness and order in the settlements;
4) the transformation of this model in neighboring states and other countries;
5) the emergence of a modern system of waste-free production in the country;
6) the development of exports of new machinery and equipment;
7) improving the ratings of the country in the field of preserving the purity and order of the environment and others.

To ensure effective work, the state, as the main interested body, and the initiator of the project should arrange effective work on:
1) monitoring and control;
2) study of foreign experience;
3) statistical analysis and accessibility of the population;
4) provision of benefits and subsidies to organizations involved in the collection, sorting, transportation and processing of HIW;
5) the organization of various preventive measures and joint social projects involving all participants in the HIW chain;
6) the system of penalties and fines for violations with the treatment and placement of HIW in the wrong places;
7) effective joint-stock management of joint organizations with a mixed form of ownership;
8) stimulating the growth of research results in the field of processing of HIW;
9) stimulating the creation of an effective chain of production and export of finished goods and equipment in the field of collecting, sorting and processing of HIW.
10) the ongoing process of education and training about the work, handling, sorting and placement of HIW.

SUPERVISORY AND MONITORING AUTHORITIES (SMA)

Supervision and control bodies are:
1) the prosecution authorities;
2) law enforcement agencies;
3) Agency of Statistics;
4) the services of the Ministry of Health;
5) services of the Ministry of Ecology and the Environment and other ministries;
6) units of local government bodies.
7) special services of enterprises and organizations.

The activities of these services will be:
1) collection of information and statistics;
2) a comparative analysis of regions, countries;
3) control of placement of HIW in the wrong places;
4) continuous monitoring;
5) the organization of preventive measures;
6) organization of joint events;
7) detection of violations;
8) the punishment of offenders or the transfer of cases to judicial bodies.

DUMPS FOR HOUSEHOLD AND INDUSTRY WASTE (HIWD)

The purpose of creating a waste-free economy is to minimize the HIW, which are transported to the HIWD.

The phased achievement of the objectives of this concept assumes that the HIWD will continue for another 5-15 years, as a place for transporting mixed HIW.

As conditions and formations of a corresponding mindset are created in the population with working with HIW, the HIWD will gradually acquire territories for sorting and processing the HIW.

Available HIWD of cities should be gradually cleared and acquire a new look. For this, at the first stage, on the territory of the HIWD it is necessary to provide not only the placement of processing equipment and machines, but also sorting.

PLACES NOT DESIGNATED FOR WASTE (PND)

Any places other than specially designed tanks and containers, automats or points of reception of HIW should be included as the places not designated for the release of HIW.

For throwing of HIW from the windows of moving objects all citizens, who are in transport, should feel the responsibility.

For the release of HIW in the wrong place, regardless of social status, compulsory punishments and fines should be provided.

For example, in Singapore, a citizen, regardless of the status, is forced to clean the streets for a whole day for throwing out the remains of a smoked cigarette or food residues in the wrong place.

In order to foster a high level of morality and social responsibility, starting with the school curriculum, special lessons should be included on the treatment of HIW. In addition, constant social advertising and TV shows on television and in the press will create a sense of citizens' responsibility for cleanliness, order and a healthy lifestyle. On the streets, special posters and billboards should also be provided as permanent reminders of the responsibility and for achieving high goals of the state in growing the thinking about economics, purity, organization and order.

MARKING AND SYMBOLS

Effective handling of HIW in each chain of the business cycle requires mutual approval of labeling and symbols with all participants of the HIW business chain.

Marking and symbols should be convenient for all categories of citizens and enterprises, including citizens with disabilities.

Marking and designation for HIW on products and goods should differ in: 1) color; 2) sensitive and visible symbols (for persons with limited vision).

In order to import goods and products from other countries, enterprises will also have to agree on all necessary markings and designations for HIW.

The producers, in turn, must agree on the color and designations for HIW with all participants in the business cycle. For illustration, consider the figure below with markings and symbols for HIW, which are placed (stamped) in color tanks and containers.

The Figure 12 shows, for example, HIW are divided into six types: 1) food HIW; 2) HIW made of wood and paper; 3) HIW from steel and iron; 4) plastic HIW; 5) HIW from fabric, and 6) mixed HIW.

These designations should be on the label of products and goods. In addition, the marked symbols, in the form of Latin symbols, in the figure will create convenience for persons with limited eye disability when determining HIW.

Figure 12 Marking HIW Bins

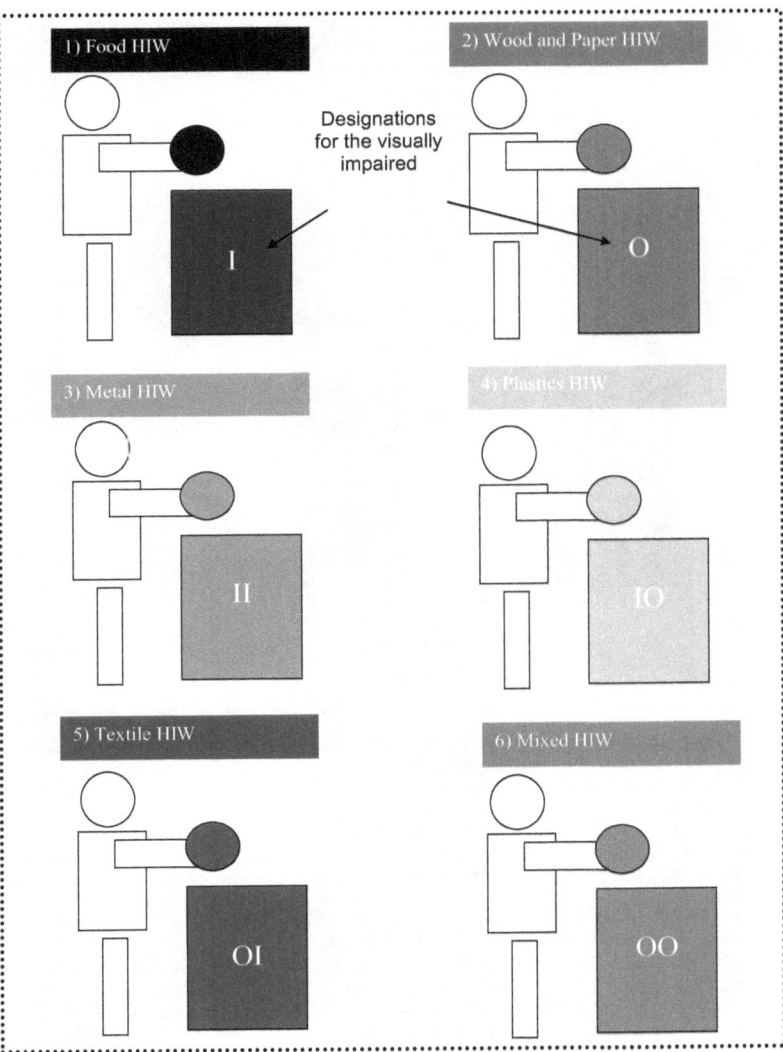

The Figure 12 above does not cover HIW made of glass, which in turn may be of different color.

From the German experience, the streets and residential areas should be placed in one large container with the ability to sort the glass by color. Consider further the Figure 12 for the placement of HIW glass.

Figure 13 Bins for Glass HIW

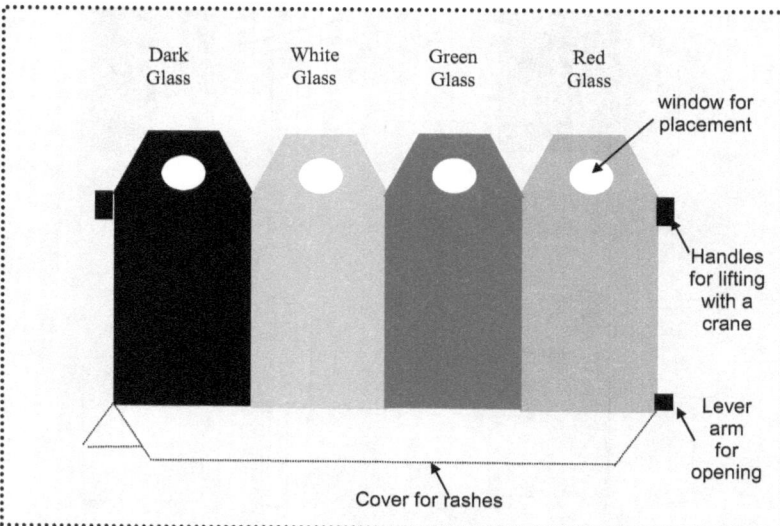

From the Figure 13 it is clear that the glass container will have different colors for the placement of glasses of different colors.

Container for placement should have a round hole for careful placement of glass (and so that citizens could not pull the glass out of the container). The container will also have special handles for the convenience of lifting with a special crane. To open the bottom cover for taking the glass out into a special transport, the container must have a lower lever that automatically opens the cover when placing the container on the special transport.

In addition, the marking must be done for: 1) HIW, which can be passed through machines; 2) HIW, which can be handed over only to HIW reception points; 3) HIW, which can be passed through trading companies; 4) HIW, which is not recommended to be placed in containers and tanks; 5) radioactive HIW; 6) poisonous HIW; 7) HIW, which requires to pass to the manufacturer through the points of reception; 8) HIW, which must be placed in special packages before being handed over or placed in containers.

Further, let's consider the preliminary markings in the following Figure 14.

Figure 14 Marking Notes for HIW Bins

1) HIW for AM

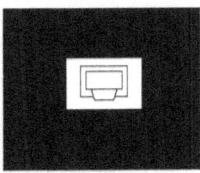

2) HIW only for reception points

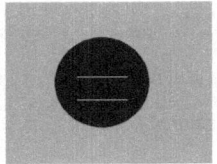

3) Returnable to shopping centers

4) It is not recommended to place in containers

5) Radioactive HIW

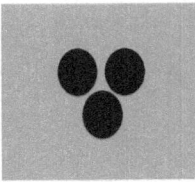

6) Poisonous HIW

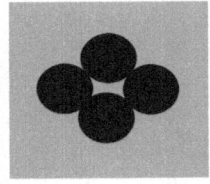

7) Returned HIW to the manufacturer

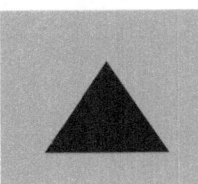

8) Require special packaging

Figure 14 shows the markings on the packaging of products that represent a convenience for recognizing HIW and their correct placement in containers or delivery to receiving points.

In addition, vehicles and uniforms of specialists, who are working with HIW should be specially labeled in categories that should be visible to the public and supervisory authorities.

All markings are not fixed and are subject to change.

Next, we will proceed to the work of public services and enterprises, and then we will consider the system of activities for factories and plants for the processing or disposal of HIW.

V - LOGISTICS

CHARACTERISTICS OF THE HUMAN SETTLEMENTS

In order to effectively locate processing plants and factories, it is necessary to examine in detail the potential of areas to locate factories and plants. But first, let's look at some of the characteristics of settlements (Table 5).

Table 5 Classification of Human Settlements for HIW

Name	Cities	Rural Areas	Village
HIW Volume	High	Low	Low
Service of the population and enterprises	Weekly	Weekly/No	Weekly
Convenience of transportation	All types of transport	Rail, auto	Rail, auto (neither)
Quantity of special transport	Many	Several	One for several regions
Placement of warehouses, reception points, logistics centers	Yes, big	Yes, medium	no
Location of processing plants	one large in several areas for each type of HIW	No	no
The average distance between settlements (km)	500 – 750	100 - 150	50 - 75
Wear equipment under current conditions	Low	Medium	High

It should be noted that in the existing landfills around major cities, HIW processing plants and factories can be located.

For effective implementation of plants and factories, we consider several scenarios from the perspective of the current situation (Table 6).

Table 6 Scenarios for Development of HIW processing infrastructure

Stage	Option 1	Option 2	Option 3
1	Restructuring of landfills and current HIW plants	Restructuring of landfills and current HIW plants, equipment upgrades	Restructuring of landfills and current HIW plants, equipment upgrades
2	Placement of new equipment for processing various types of HIW	Opening of new logistics centers for HIW	Opening of new compact HIW plants and factories with the participation of interested enterprises
3	Opening of new logistics centers for HIW	Opening of new compact HIW plants and factories with the participation of interested enterprises	Opening of new logistics centers for HIW
4	Opening of new compact HIW plants and factories with the participation of interested enterprises	Expansion of activities abroad	Expansion of activities abroad
5	Expansion of activities abroad		

The choice of the best option will depend on many other factors. For example, the volume of various types of HIW, transport and infrastructure capabilities, the time to overcome long distances, and the cost of implementing projects. Consider a few of them.

1) The volume of various types of HIW. In this case, if the amount of plastic as HIW will have a large share in all regions at the same time, then, placing small compact smelting plants in each region is more expedient than organizing transportation to one large plant over a distance of 1000 kilometers.

2) Transport and infrastructure facilities. In this case, if for any processed type of HIW, channels for further implementation are not found, then the whole point of the modern HIW system is lost. To this end, research and scientific departments of factories and plants should start in advance to search for new types of products, materials or raw materials that will be in demand in the market.

3) The cost of time and resources. The time required to transport HIW from villages and rural areas to HIW plants may not be effective without creating an optimal map of HIW logistics centers in rural areas or the best route for special equipment.

SCHEME OF TRANSPORATION OF HIW TO FACTORY AND PLANTS

The movement of HIW in the chain is important for the effectiveness of the HIW system. If the movement processes are slow and tedious for workers, or it takes a huge amount of time to transport from one point to another due to the inefficient location of the HIW logistics centers, as well as the HIW processing plants, the system's capacity will be limited and regression. In addition, the quality of roads will have one of the main factors in the speed of services and the wear and tear of transport and special equipment.

Another main goal is the creation of a very flexible map of the movement of HIW, adapted to each region of the country.

Consider an example in the following Figure 15, where the arrows indicate the movement of HIW in the chain of transportation of HIW from sources of HIW to factories and plants for further processing of HIW.

Figure 15 Logistics System of HIW

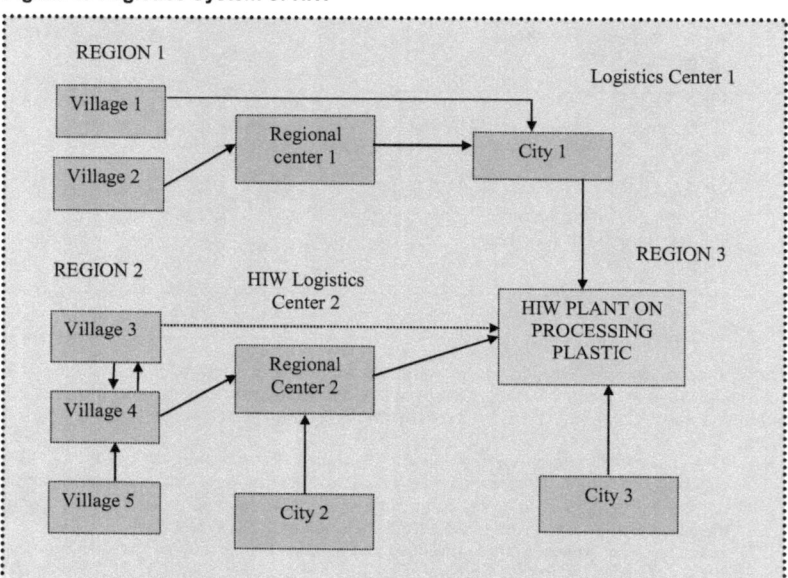

The Figure 15 shows that the movement of the HIW in the chain can be built very flexibly. For example, take the HIW movement in the first area. Due to the remoteness of the villages from each other, it may be advisable to transport HIW depending on the distance from the logistics center. For example, Village 1 is located at a greater distance from the city where the logistics center is located. On the way from the village to the city there are no other villages. Therefore, transportation from village 1 to the city where the logistics center is located is direct.

Village 2 is also located at a greater distance, but on the way to the city, a Regional Center is located here. Therefore, special transport, which follows from village 2 to the city, on the way takes the HIW from the Regional Center too.

Now consider the option with the Region 2. Here we see that the logistics center 2 is located in the Regional Center 2, and not in the city, since the district is located closer to the HIW plant for the smelting of plastics. So, the HIW gathered in all villages and transported to the Regional Center 2 and then further to the HIW Plan on Processing Plastic.

In addition, the Figure 15 shows that from village 1, the dotted line points the arrow of the movement of HIW directly to the plastic smelting plant. This variant of the route depends on the route of the special transport, and on the volume of the collected HIW. If the special transport, coming from the village 3 to village 2 knows through the navigation system information that with cargo volume in village 1 the special transport will be full, then the route of the special transport will be through village 1 to the HIW processing plant.

In general, a system can be very flexible and efficient only by optimally constructing a route and a HIW system, using an info-communication and navigation systems.

SCHEME OF HIW PLANTS AND FACTORIES

For the effective use of space and resources, it is necessary to pay attention to the internal location of various objects of HIW plants and factories. For illustration, I will try to give several options.

Option 1. In the Figure 16 below you can see the layout of a large plant (factory) for processing one type of HIW.

Figure 16 Layout of Plant for Processing of one type of HIW

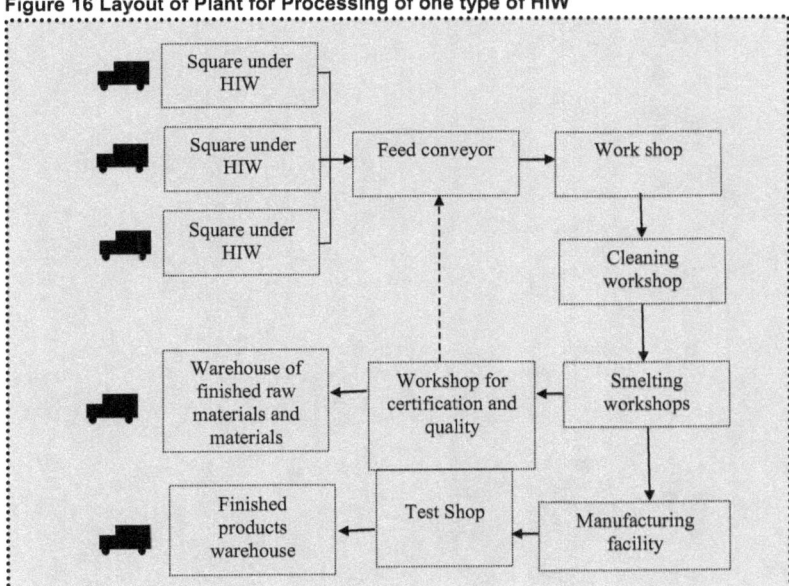

45

It can be seen from the Figure 16 that the placement of the workshops of the plant is optimally located. All warehouses and areas are located on the one hand, and smelting shops and production shops, on the other.

In addition, the Figure 16 shows that the HIW plant not only produces final raw materials or materials, but also has a production department, which, at the request of customers, produces certain products. The demand for raw materials and materials, as well as products, depends on the activity of the scientific and technical research activities over the HIW of the plant.

It also shows that the products failed to pass certification and returned to the conveyer for smelting.

Option 2. Consider the layout of a large processing plant for several types of HIW or the entire range of HIW (Figure 17).

Figure 17 Layout of Plant for Processing of several types of HIW

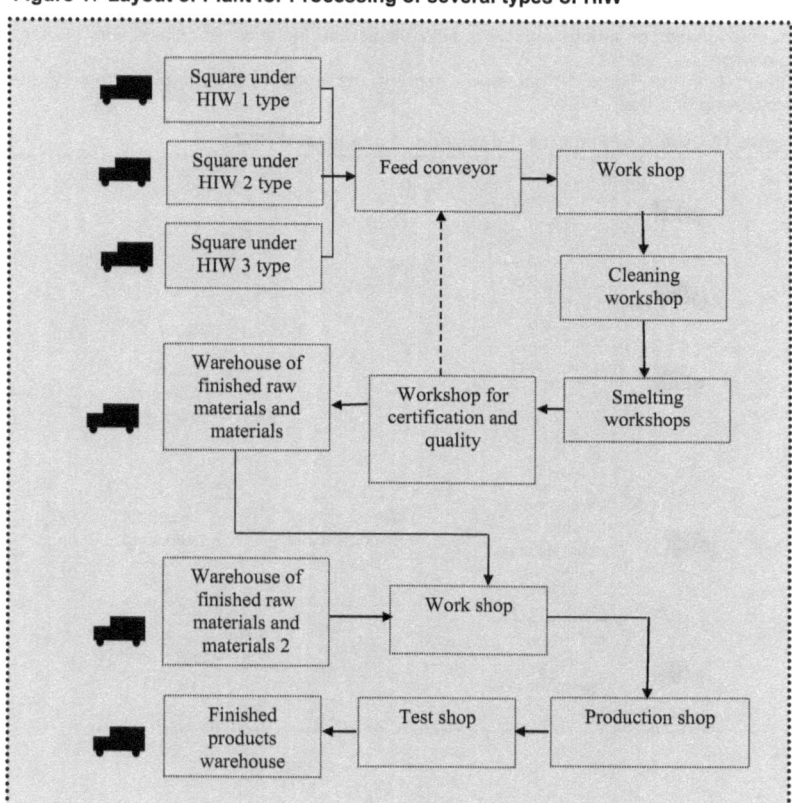

The Figure 17 shows a chain of processes for several types of HIW. And it shows that, respectively, the plant can produce more complex products, or sell finished raw materials or reprocess HIW further to product finished goods and products.

XI - BENEFITS AND INCOME

The benefits and revenues from the implementation of projects for the development of HIW management systems are unlimited. The following Figure 18 shows the main benefits and revenues of country in the macroeconomic sphere.

Figure 18 Benefits and Revenues of the Country from HIW processing

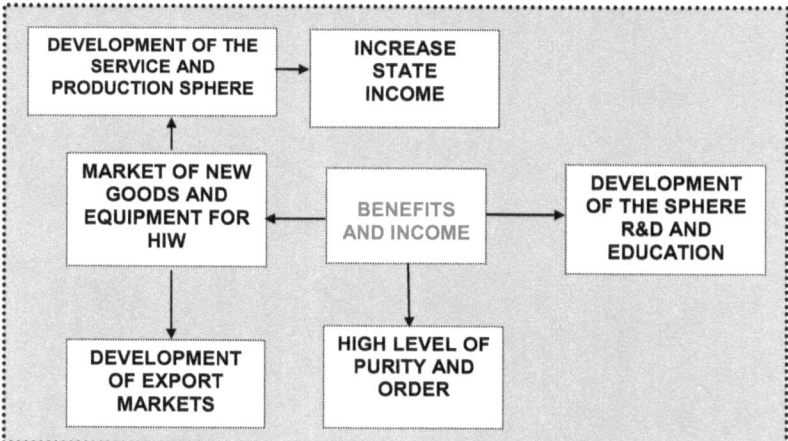

The advantage of the development of high-tech equipment, machinery and equipment in the field of HIW management system is one of the important areas of development, and should be one of the priority areas. It is important that the prioritization of this area includes:

1) development in the population the desire to research and develop, continuously improve skills, get new education, change in thinking and resolve life issues (work, leisure, sports, social event, family planning, education) to prioritize the creation and implementation of government goals.
2) understanding of the rules for activities and working of developed economies;
3) understanding of large and neighboring markets for consumption of high-tech products and goods: Europe, China, Uzbekistan, Iran, India, Pakistan, etc.
4) understanding and knowledge of R&D markets, patents and licenses for intellectual values and property;
5) understanding and knowledge of languages, culture, perception, and most importantly, labeling of goods and products for the effective export of equipment, machinery and equipment to target regions;
6) understanding and knowledge of the capacities of own production and sales markets for quick adaptation of production capabilities in case of changing the volume of demand for products abroad;
7) development of the R&D sphere with specific objectives and goals to achieve, with a focus on time, budget and personnel;

8) building an effective process and cycle of R&D, planning, production, testing and launching the results to the market;
9) the main motivational factor of the population and youth to high-tech specialties is an increase of the role by the state and enterprises for income and well-being of people engaged in R&D and education in all areas that contribute to the development of innovations in the economy.

A) SOCIAL - ECONOMIC BENEFITS FOR THE STATE

Effective HIW management system and chain of activities can increase employment in the country manifolds.

The increase in taxes to the state treasury from the activity of the HIW chain will be also tremendous.

In addition, the waste management activities are directly related to the improvement of cleanliness and order in settlements and cities, reduction of costs for maintaining cleanliness, improving the sphere of R&D, public thinking, the development of HIW infrastructure, new ICT products and services, production and the development of the export potential of the country.

B) SUPPORTING GROUPS

To implement the project for the development of the HIW chain, it is necessary that not only the state and the private sector are concerned be at the center of the project implementation. The main support group of the HIW management projects should be also the following groups:

1) Mass media (headings, TV shows, articles, etc.);
2) Professional communication sector (navigation, professional communication, etc.);
3) The telecommunications and information technology sector (software, communications, the Internet, etc.);
4) The advertising sector (social advertising in the media and the press, street billboards, etc.);
5) Independent public foundations, political parties, state public foundations, institutions and organizations (joint-stock management, social and preventive measures, seminars, conferences, competitions, etc.);
6) Educational institutions (joint-stock management, training programs, courses, trainings, seminars and trainings);
7) Law enforcement and supervisory and control authorities (video monitoring of the area, detection of violators, preventive measures, fines and arrests);
8) R&D institutions, independent and private designers, researchers, architects, designers (joint-stock management, marketing, laboratory work, design and calculations of equipment, machines, equipment, tanks, containers, transport, infrastructure, etc.);
9) Manufacturing enterprises and the private sector 1 (joint-stock management, production of equipment, machinery, equipment, tanks, containers, transport, infrastructure, etc.);

10) Enterprises and the private service sector 2 (joint-stock management, organization, calculations and implementation of projects, monitoring, consulting, control, export);

11) Foreign and local investors (joint-stock management, investment, transfer of knowledge and experience, etc.);

12) Foreign and local scientists and professors, students, trainees, trainees (participation in projects);

13) Independent organizations, volunteers, trainees and trainees (educational activities, setting up work processes for collecting, sorting, transporting and processing HIW, cleaning works).

C) GLOBAL ENVIRONMENT

With the successful implementation of the project and the achievement of a certain level of production capacity for the transportation of HIW equipment, machinery and equipment, a country can become not only the global initiator of HIW projects, but also one of the leading countries in the field of knowledge, experience and technology.

With the correct arrangement of work on the action plan for the implementation of the global HIW project, a country can become the initiator of the following global projects:

1) opening of a global center and headquarters for the study and solutions in the field of HIW trends, problems and innovations;

2) starting of a global database on HIW researchers: in space, airspace, underground, on land and water;

3) launch of a global database of HIW plants and factories around the world;

4) organization of a center for the association of public foundations and organizations working in the field of HIW;

5) creation of the center for coordination and development of the global projects in the field of HIW.

These initiatives allow not only to expand the image of the country, increase tourists, but mainly in improving the global environment and climate.

X – ACTION PLAN

A) GENERAL PLAN

Stages	Activities	Costs	Responsible	Results	Deadlines
1	Further study and research of data	Budget	Government, Institutions	Statistics, Outcomes and Conclusions	3-6 month
2	Planning and calculation	Budget	Government	Number of projects, Budget, Participants	3-6 month
3	Organization and coordination of projects	Budget	Government, Private Sector	Ready projects, Participants, Deadlines, Responsible people	3-6 month
4	Project	Budget	Government,	Socio-	1- 10 year

	Realization		Private Sector, Public Sector	economic effects, Statistics	
5	Monitoring and Control	Budget	Government, Institutions	Statistics, Coefficient	constantly

B) TARGET PROJECTS

#	Projects	Responsible	Budget and Deadlines
1	R&D	Government, Private Sector	constantly, and for each project in detail
2	Project Preparation	Government, Private Sector	for each project
3	ICT projects	Government, Private Sector	for each project
4	Education and Training	Government, Private Sector	constantly, and for each project in detail
5	Production	Government, Private Sector	for each project
6	Service: collection, sorting, transportation.	Government, Private Sector	for each project
7	HIW plants: processing and production of finished products	Government, Private Sector	for each project
8	Standards, labeling and designation	Government	for each project
9	Preventive and social events, social advertising, conferences and seminars	Government, Private Sector	constantly
10	Monitoring and control systems	Government, Private Sector	constantly

C) DEVELOPMENT OF PRODUCTION

#	Activities	Responsible	Budget	Deadlines
1	Study of foreign countries, the definition of market niches	Institutions	Government, Private Sector	constantly
2	R&D	Institutions	Government, Private Sector	constantly
3	Planning and product design for the HIW industry	Enterprises	Government, Private Sector	Till 1 month
4	Search for investment to start production	Enterprises	Government, Private Sector	Till 1 month
5	Project implementation	Enterprises	Private Sector, Government	From 1 month till 1years

| 6 | Production of HIW equipment, machinery and equipment | Enterprises | Private Sector | From 3 months till 1years |
| 7 | Export of HIW equipment, machinery and equipment | Enterprises | Private Sector | - |

D) IMAGE DEVELOPMENT

#	Activities	Responsible	Budget	Deadlines
1	Market research and definition of topics for meetings, seminars, forums in the field of HIW	State bodies, NGO, NGF	mixed	From 1 month till 1 year
2	Organization of seminars, forums, etc.	State bodies, NGO, NGF	mixed	From 1 moth till 1 year
3	Advertising and promotion of ideas	State bodies, NGO, NGF	mixed	Before organizing a seminar, forum, etc.
4	Formation of initiatives to open centers with the invitation of world scientists, etc.	Private		During a seminar, forum, etc.
5	Presentation of ideas, concepts and projects	State bodies, NGO, NGF		During a seminar, forum, etc..
6	Implementation of ideas, concepts and projects with the involvement of the global community	Joint projects	mixed	From 1 year till 10 years

XI – RULES OF WORK AND HANDLING OF HIW

POPULATION AND ENTERPRISES

To work effectively with HIW, it is necessary that every citizen or enterprise, who are direct sources of HIW, observe the following basic rules for handling HIW:

1) place HIW in containers according to the specified designations and markings;
2) clean HIW from dirt, dust, food debris etc.;
3) comply with the rules for handling the packaging of liquid, food and hazardous HIW;
4) when it is difficult to determine HIW, take them to special reception points by telephone or from HIW;
5) when it is difficult to determine HIW in a flying or moving object, contact to the board conductors;
6) comply with the rules of placement in containers, tanks, automatic machines;
7) do not leave the remains of vital activity in public, natural places;
8) do not throw the HIW from the vehicle;
9) do not burn HIW in private territories and premises;
10) do not bury HIW in private territories and premises;
11) do not smoke in public places, but in strictly designated areas;
12) increase the culture of work and treatment with HIW etc.

SERVICE ORGANIZATIONS

1) employees' uniforms and transport have to have special markings and symbols to notice at different times of the day and from a distance;
2) employees comply with the rules for receiving, transporting, storing, loading and unloading various types of HIW;
3) any employee at any time should provide effective advice to the public and enterprises;
4) transport staff must decide and change the route depending on the volume, types of HIW, distance between settlements etc.;
5) service companies have to have an effective navigation and communication system;
6) maintenance services should have an effective vehicle monitoring system.
7) employees of equipment and transport should use all available resources economically.
8) must comply with all state and environmental standards;
9) must conduct laboratory and scientific research;
10) increased the level and quality of services to the population and enterprises and others.

HIW PLANTS AND FACTORIES

1) plants and factories must comply with all environmental and environmental standards;
2) must constantly update the fleet of equipment and technology for the effective and high-quality processing of HIW;
3) must conduct research and development together with manufacturing enterprises for the production of new types of products and goods;

4) employees and equipment must use production resources economically;
5) must respond flexibly to changes in the volume of processing of HIW and others.

CONCLUSION

The introduction of projects in the country in the field of HIW under the slogan "for cleanliness and economy" will be the first step before a country initiates a global project on HIW, which will make it possible to effectively use of our limited resources of the planet and to effectively reach the level of zero waste around the world.

Waste Management should become a new trend in all corners of our planet and especially in for all countries in cleaning our oceans and uninhabited places.

Today, the majority of enterprises and organizations in the world produce products and goods only to meet consumer demand, and final consumers do not always think about how they could play a key role in saving resources, reducing the cost of products and goods if consumers (on time, periodically and organized) handed over HIW or exchanged them for new products and services. After all, we see how many unnecessary goods, products, things are around us and they are now in our homes, cottages, garages, oceans and even already in space.

The population and enterprises, as a consumer of goods and services, and at the same time as a source of HIW, not only create a threat to their existence on Earth, but already go out into the open space. Imagine that obsolete or outdated space objects will constantly fall from the sky onto populated areas, or new spacecraft flying into space will constantly collide with space HIW.

On the earth's surface, even now many species of plant and animal life are simply dying, even where people are practically absent. The action of the HIW makes itself felt, and perhaps humanity still does not understand how the human race itself is gradually and gradually killed by the waste.

It is necessary to take cardinal and effective measures to create a mechanism for efficient processing of waste in almost all countries of the world.

We believe that the state and financial institutions of our communities support the implementation of the concept and deeply believe that this will allow a country to take one of the first initiatives and a global responsibility in promoting cleanliness and saving resources through effective waste management.

NOTES AND MEMORIES

Where can you find interesting stories about investments, export and trade on the internet?

Nurbek Achilov has some resources for you!

On Blogger's platform he runs his blog about investments, export, trade and other issues.

Blog about investment, export and trade in English:
https://nurbekachilov.blogspot.com/

Blog about investment, export and trade in English:
https://nurbekachil.blogspot.com/

You can also find ideas, photos and experiences about investments, trade and investment on Nurbek Achilov's pages in Facebook, Instagram, Pinterest, Slideshare, Academia and LinkedIn and other accounts.
orcid.org/0000-0003-1238-6556

Get the Second Edition with the Special Price on Amazon.com

Kazakhstan

Tips for Travelers

Nurbek Achilov

Second Edition

Get my new book with the Special Price on Amazon.com

200 web-sites and tools for online presence

Essential Handbook for marketing and growth

Nurbek Achilov

First Edition

Get the Second Edition with the Special Price on Amazon.com

Handbook for Marketing Students

Best tips and strategies

Nurbek Achilov

First Edition

Get the Second Edition with the Special Price on Amazon.com

EVENT MANAGEMENT

Tips and strategies

Nigel Aksel

Second Edition